I0762720

TO
FROM
DATE

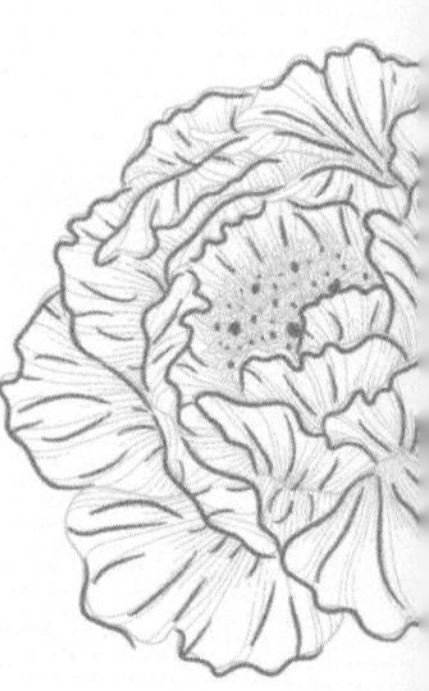

PRAYER JOURNAL FOR *Moms*

DaySpring
LIVE YOUR FAITH

Introduction

From the moment you learned you were going to be a mother, you knew your life would never be the same! God chose you to be a parent to those precious young ones you call "son" or "daughter," and He has a plan for your lives that He is working out day by day by day. Motherhood—there's nothing like it. It is a divine calling that shapes lives, nurtures souls, and reveals the depth of a love that knows no bounds. For moms, each day is a journey filled with joy, challenges, laughter, tears, and an unyielding desire to give their best to their children and families. In the midst of this beautiful chaos, it is essential for mothers to find solace, strength, and spiritual nourishment to navigate the various seasons of motherhood with faith and grace.

Within the pages of this book, mothers will find a sanctuary where they can pause, reflect, and connect with their Creator amidst the demands of daily life. It is important to stay grounded in the Word of God throughout the joys and struggles of motherhood, for it alone can provide the reassurance moms need to move past moments of doubt, the inspiration needed during times of exhaustion, and the constant reminder that God is always there, ready to steady the feet of those He has called to this sacred journey of motherhood.

God has a plan for you, dearest mom. As you embrace the joyous and challenging moments of motherhood with grace, you can begin to view them as opportunities for spiritual growth. During those quiet moments when you spend time with the Lord, allow Him to be your most cherished companion, as He reminds you to lay down your burdens, rest in Him, and remember how valued you are by your heavenly Father. As you delve into the devotions and Scriptures found on these pages, may you be embraced by the all-encompassing grace of God, finding strength, wisdom, and joy in every grace-filled moment of motherhood.

The Power of a Praying Mom

The idea of being fully responsible for another, smaller human can be overwhelming. Some days, getting out of bed and possibly taking a shower, feeding the kids, and making sure they are safe—these are the things you're most proud of. But one of the most powerful things a mom can do for her children is pray for them. Every day, from the time your child was in the womb to long into adulthood, your prayers regarding your children are acknowledged before God.

No one in the world sees your children like you do. No one can pray with the same insights or observations. And a mother's prayer certainly blesses God's heart. After all, He invites us as parents to communicate the same selfless love that He has for us. And because He knows we're ill equipped to do that apart from Him, He makes Himself highly available for that very purpose. As we seek Him in motherhood, He pours out His most fatherly love over us and our families. He puts other women in our lives who can love, mentor, encourage, and build us up on the adventure. He helps us with creative problem-solving, enduring late nights, and giving more grace than we can measure.

Prayer is effective because He not only listens to us, but He also responds and tells us His secrets. Jeremiah 33:3 (ESV) says, "Call to me and I will answer you, and will tell you great and hidden things that you have not known." What He desires from us is a relationship. When we seek Him out for wisdom, He promises to give it. When we trust Him in our unknowns, He promises that He is our Light.

As the Artist and Creator of your child, He put every single cell together in a very intentional way. Your child's genetic makeup, including their likes and dislikes, quirks and strengths, passions and purpose are all recorded in His notes. He can give you one-of-a-kind direction on how to shepherd your child through their lives. Remember, He chose your child for such a time as this. (He chose you for such a time too!) So there's no better place to turn than to your loving Father when it comes to navigating the hard nights, the temper tantrums, the difficult choices, the ever-growing to-do list, the confusing pick-up and drop-off schedules, as well as *anything* you will *ever* face as a mom. He will guide you through it all.

DATE

Dear God

Today, I am grateful for . . .

My heart's prayer for my child(ren) is . . .

Worries I need to surrender to You . . .

I am feeling overloaded with . . .

Grant me Your unwavering strength for . . .

Fill me with Your wisdom as I seek understanding in . . .

In Jesus's Name. Amen.

But those who trust the LORD will find new strength.
They will be strong like eagles soaring upward on wings;
they will walk and run without getting tired.

ISAIAH 40:31 CEV

DATE

Dear God

Today, I am grateful for . . .

My heart's prayer for my child(ren) is . . .

Worries I need to surrender to You . . .

I am feeling overloaded with . . .

Grant me Your unwavering strength for . . .

Fill me with Your wisdom as I seek understanding in . . .

In Jesus's Name. Amen.

"Come to me, all who labor and are heavy laden,
and I will give you rest."
MATTHEW 11:28 ESV

DATE

Dear God

Today, I am grateful for . . .

My heart's prayer for my child(ren) is . . .

Worries I need to surrender to You . . .

I am feeling overloaded with . . .

Grant me Your unwavering strength for . . .

Fill me with Your wisdom as I seek understanding in . . .

In Jesus's Name. Amen.

If any of you lacks wisdom, you should ask God,
who gives generously to all without finding fault, and it will be given to you.

James 1:5 niv

DATE

Dear God

Today, I am grateful for . . .

My heart's prayer for my child(ren) is . . .

Worries I need to surrender to You . . .

I am feeling overloaded with . . .

Grant me Your unwavering strength for . . .

Fill me with Your wisdom as I seek understanding in . . .

In Jesus's Name. Amen.

He leads the humble in doing right,
teaching them His way.
Psalm 25:9 NLT

DATE

Dear God

Today, I am grateful for . . .

My heart's prayer for my child(ren) is . . .

Worries I need to surrender to You . . .

I am feeling overloaded with . . .

Grant me Your unwavering strength for . . .

Fill me with Your wisdom as I seek understanding in . . .

In Jesus's Name. Amen.

"If you abide in Me, and My words abide in you,
you will ask what you desire, and it shall be done for you."

John 15:7 nkjv

DATE

Dear God

Today, I am grateful for . . .

My heart's prayer for my child(ren) is . . .

Worries I need to surrender to You . . .

I am feeling overloaded with . . .

Grant me Your unwavering strength for . . .

Fill me with Your wisdom as I seek understanding in . . .

In Jesus's Name. Amen.

Pray without ceasing.

I Thessalonians 5:17 esv

DATE

Dear God

Today, I am grateful for . . .

My heart's prayer for my child(ren) is . . .

Worries I need to surrender to You . . .

I am feeling overloaded with . . .

Grant me Your unwavering strength for . . .

Fill me with Your wisdom as I seek understanding in . . .

In Jesus's Name. Amen.

Don't worry about anything, but pray about everything.
With thankful hearts offer up your prayers and requests to God.

PHILIPPIANS 4:6 CEV

Childlike Trust

Parenting is a delicate balance between protecting our kids and letting them take risks to learn and grow. But one thing we must never compromise on, as much as it depends on us, is their safety. Some children are naturally cautious. Others are of the "leap first, look second" variety. Regardless, as moms we often have a bird's-eye view of the situation our children are in, and we can guide them safely through their surroundings.

Whether they realize it or not, our kids trust us. Even as babies, our children don't worry about being fed, changed, or snuggled. Your toddler doesn't consider whether it's a good idea to suck on the dog's squeaky toy, or whether it's safe to climb the nearest chair and reach for an object high on a shelf. At this young stage, children trust their moms to be there no matter what. And often, they don't even see the danger they could be in. They get upset that something is taken away from them. They are so caught up in themselves—discovering and exploring—that it often takes the more experienced eye to guide their process. In fact, it's the childlike faith in us, their parents and protectors, that allows them to live freely and discover the world around them.

As adults, we are invited into a childlike faith. Jesus said, "Truly I tell you, unless you change and become like little children, you will never enter the kingdom of heaven. Therefore, whoever takes the lowly position of this child is the greatest in the kingdom of heaven. And whoever welcomes one such child in My name welcomes Me" (Matthew 18:3–5 NIV). Jesus iterates to us that trusting Him—freely, joyfully, and adventurously—is the way to live life to the full.

Our heavenly Father takes on the role of our Protector and Shepherd. He sees our surroundings and knows what is best for us. And as mothers, the more freely we rely on Him to keep us secure in Him as we focus on guiding our kids, the more we will learn to enjoy our role as moms.

Just as babies will turn to their parents when they recognize the need, we can turn to God as often as we need. He is our shield, our help, and our most trustworthy Father. And He wants nothing more than to love us with His everlasting love.

DATE

Dear God

Today, I am grateful for . . .

My heart's prayer for my child(ren) is . . .

Worries I need to surrender to You . . .

I am feeling overloaded with . . .

Grant me Your unwavering strength for . . .

Fill me with Your wisdom as I seek understanding in . . .

In Jesus's Name. Amen.

"Let the little children come to me and do not hinder them,
for to such belongs the kingdom of heaven."
MATTHEW 19:14 ESV

DATE

Dear God

Today, I am grateful for . . .

My heart's prayer for my child(ren) is . . .

Worries I need to surrender to You . . .

I am feeling overloaded with . . .

Grant me Your unwavering strength for . . .

Fill me with Your wisdom as I seek understanding in . . .

In Jesus's Name. Amen.

"You have taught children
and infants to give You praise."
MATTHEW 21:16 NLT

DATE

Dear God

Today, I am grateful for . . .

My heart's prayer for my child(ren) is . . .

Worries I need to surrender to You . . .

I am feeling overloaded with . . .

Grant me Your unwavering strength for . . .

Fill me with Your wisdom as I seek understanding in . . .

In Jesus's Name. Amen.

We put our hope in the LORD.
He is our help and our shield.
PSALM 33:20 NLT

DATE

Dear God

Today, I am grateful for . . .

My heart's prayer for my child(ren) is . . .

Worries I need to surrender to You . . .

I am feeling overloaded with . . .

Grant me Your unwavering strength for . . .

Fill me with Your wisdom as I seek understanding in . . .

In Jesus's Name. Amen.

Without faith it is impossible to please God,
because anyone who comes to Him must believe
that He exists and that He rewards those who earnestly seek Him.

Hebrews 11:6 niv

DATE

Dear God

Today, I am grateful for . . .

My heart's prayer for my child(ren) is . . .

Worries I need to surrender to You . . .

I am feeling overloaded with . . .

Grant me Your unwavering strength for . . .

Fill me with Your wisdom as I seek understanding in . . .

In Jesus's Name. Amen.

Yet some people accepted Him and put their faith in Him.
So He gave them the right to be the children of God.

John 1:12 CEV

DATE

Dear God

Today, I am grateful for . . .

My heart's prayer for my child(ren) is . . .

Worries I need to surrender to You . . .

I am feeling overloaded with . . .

Grant me Your unwavering strength for . . .

Fill me with Your wisdom as I seek understanding in . . .

In Jesus's Name. Amen.

Peace be within your walls
and security within your towers!
PSALM 122:7 ESV

DATE

Dear God

Today, I am grateful for . . .

My heart's prayer for my child(ren) is . . .

Worries I need to surrender to You . . .

I am feeling overloaded with . . .

Grant me Your unwavering strength for . . .

Fill me with Your wisdom as I seek understanding in . . .

In Jesus's Name. Amen.

The LORD is my strength and my shield;
my heart trusts in Him, and He helps me.

PSALM 28:7 NIV

Created for This

Social media is quick to tell us that we just don't compare to other moms. By the look of their kids, puppies, and sunny vacations, everyone else's lives are nearly perfect. As you scroll along, enviously noting their perfectly placed pillows, masterfully plated meals, expertly organized closets, and well-behaved siblings—you glance up at the dish-filled sink and crumb-covered counter. You notice the baby left a vomit stain on your shoulder, and you forgot to change your shirt before the video call you had for work. Your toddler screams in the corner because you cut his sandwich into squares instead of triangles. Your grade-schooler forgot about the bake sale, and so you're scrambling to create five dozen cookies by tomorrow morning. Your teenager barely looks up from the screen or adamantly refuses to say "thank you." Whatever other people are doing, you feel like you weren't cut out to be a mom on some days.

The truth is, people rarely memorialize the less-than-perfect times on their social media pages. And in much the same way, the world rarely sees the insecurities and worries we face every time we lay our head on the pillow at night. We judge others by their neatly trimmed outer lives, and we judge ourselves by our messy, disorganized, emotional insides. That, friend, is not apples to apples.

But the greater truth? You. Are. Enough. There is no better mother for your child than you. No one's education would make them raise your child with more beneficial expertise. No one's hug would feel better to your child than yours. No one's broccoli cuts or buttered noodles would taste better to your child—not really. Because you were created for this family, for this time, for this child.

Ephesians 2:10 reminds us that "we are God's handiwork, created in Christ Jesus to do good works, which God prepared in advance for us to do" (NIV). You know what that means? God has designed you for motherhood. All of its messes and memories, supreme joys and crocodile tears and special celebrations. He has prepared you perfectly, even if it doesn't look at all perfect. You've got this. Because He has you.

Sure—everyone can learn and grow. There may be books worth reading and experts worth following. There are friends or family members worth observing in their strengths as parents. But what your child needs most is the vessel through which all that love was made to be channeled—YOU.

Don't let anyone ever tell you that being a mom isn't a ministry or a purpose. As you pour into your kids, He will pour into you. He prepared you for this family, and He prepared this family for you. Your child will thrive as you share yourself—your whole, imperfect, beautiful self.

DATE

Dear God

Today, I am grateful for . . .

My heart's prayer for my child(ren) is . . .

Worries I need to surrender to You . . .

I am feeling overloaded with . . .

Grant me Your unwavering strength for . . .

Fill me with Your wisdom as I seek understanding in . . .

In Jesus's Name. Amen.

Obviously, I'm not trying to win the approval of people, but of God. If pleasing people were my goal, I would not be Christ's servant.

GALATIANS 1:10 NLT

DATE

Dear God

Today, I am grateful for . . .

My heart's prayer for my child(ren) is . . .

Worries I need to surrender to You . . .

I am feeling overloaded with . . .

Grant me Your unwavering strength for . . .

Fill me with Your wisdom as I seek understanding in . . .

In Jesus's Name. Amen.

But let each one test his own work, and then his reason to boast
will be in himself alone and not in his neighbor.

Galatians 6:4 ESV

DATE

Dear God

Today, I am grateful for . . .

My heart's prayer for my child(ren) is . . .

Worries I need to surrender to You . . .

I am feeling overloaded with . . .

Grant me Your unwavering strength for . . .

Fill me with Your wisdom as I seek understanding in . . .

In Jesus's Name. Amen.

Do nothing out of selfish ambition or vain conceit.
Rather, in humility value others above yourselves,
not looking to your own interests but each of you to the interests of the others.

PHILIPPIANS 2:3–4 NIV

DATE

Dear God

Today, I am grateful for . . .

My heart's prayer for my child(ren) is . . .

Worries I need to surrender to You . . .

I am feeling overloaded with . . .

Grant me Your unwavering strength for . . .

Fill me with Your wisdom as I seek understanding in . . .

In Jesus's Name. Amen.

Do your best to win God's approval as a worker
who doesn't need to be ashamed and who teaches only the true message.

II Timothy 2:15 CEV

DATE

Dear God

Today, I am grateful for . . .

My heart's prayer for my child(ren) is . . .

Worries I need to surrender to You . . .

I am feeling overloaded with . . .

Grant me Your unwavering strength for . . .

Fill me with Your wisdom as I seek understanding in . . .

In Jesus's Name. Amen.

"You shall not covet your neighbor's house . . .
or anything that belongs to your neighbor."

Exodus 20:17 NIV

DATE

Dear God

Today, I am grateful for . . .

My heart's prayer for my child(ren) is . . .

Worries I need to surrender to You . . .

I am feeling overloaded with . . .

Grant me Your unwavering strength for . . .

Fill me with Your wisdom as I seek understanding in . . .

In Jesus's Name. Amen.

The LORD is on my side;
I will not fear.
What can man do to me?
PSALM 118:6 ESV

DATE

Dear God

Today, I am grateful for . . .

My heart's prayer for my child(ren) is . . .

Worries I need to surrender to You . . .

I am feeling overloaded with . . .

Grant me Your unwavering strength for . . .

Fill me with Your wisdom as I seek understanding in . . .

In Jesus's Name. Amen.

When I look at the night sky and see the work of Your fingers—
the moon and the stars You set in place—what are mere mortals
that You should think about them, human beings that You should care for them?

PSALM 8:3–4 NLT

A Partner in Parenting

Motherhood comes in a blur of emotion. It's awe, at the tiny miracle wrapped in your arms. It's overwhelm, at all there is to learn and the incredible imperativeness of keeping a baby person alive under your watch. It can be loneliness—of navigating things without the help of family, or of being the only one in your age group with a child the age of yours. It can be desperation at translating the cries of a newborn, or at not knowing what to say when your child comes home in tears. It can also be joy—bursting like fireworks as your baby smiles for the first time or when that adoption finally comes through.

Nobody—repeat that: NOBODY—knows what kind of mom she'll be before she becomes one. All the observation in the world, all the social media experts, all the advice in books or over the phone, none of it can prepare a mother for her child. Because your journey is your own, you can feel so isolated. And those feelings can be exacerbated by well-meaning others assuring you that time flies, that you should enjoy it while you can—and just wait until she's a teenager or flying the coop.

There is a step you can always take, though, and that is toward God. James 4:8 promises that when we come near to Him, He will come near to us. Opening the Bible every day gives Him room to highlight truth to us or speak to us through God-breathed words. Imagine talking to God like you talk to a friend on the phone, venting your frustrations and sharing your celebrations. He is close, and He is listening. And when you need Him most, God the Comforter comes. He knows the pain of parenting better than anyone. He also knows the most extreme joy and is just waiting to jump up and down with you over parenting wins and the things that make you the happiest.

You can find confidence in this: your prayers matter to Him. He will be the first to tell you, motherhood is a series of seasons. Each season serves to grow you, mature you, enrich you, and bless you in ways beyond anything you can imagine right now. There are times in life when we walk more by faith than others. But every single step of faith that we take makes a difference—to us, and to our kids.

DATE

Dear God

Today, I am grateful for . . .

My heart's prayer for my child(ren) is . . .

Worries I need to surrender to You . . .

I am feeling overloaded with . . .

Grant me Your unwavering strength for . . .

Fill me with Your wisdom as I seek understanding in . . .

In Jesus's Name. Amen.

Come close to God,
and God will come close to you.
JAMES 4:8 NLT

DATE

Dear God

Today, I am grateful for . . .

My heart's prayer for my child(ren) is . . .

Worries I need to surrender to You . . .

I am feeling overloaded with . . .

Grant me Your unwavering strength for . . .

Fill me with Your wisdom as I seek understanding in . . .

In Jesus's Name. Amen.

"Remain in Me, as I also remain in you.
No branch can bear fruit by itself; it must remain in the vine.
Neither can you bear fruit unless you remain in Me."

John 15:4 niv

DATE

Dear God

Today, I am grateful for . . .

My heart's prayer for my child(ren) is . . .

Worries I need to surrender to You . . .

I am feeling overloaded with . . .

Grant me Your unwavering strength for . . .

Fill me with Your wisdom as I seek understanding in . . .

In Jesus's Name. Amen.

Surely God is my help;
the Lord is the One who sustains me.

Psalm 54:4 niv

DATE

Dear God

Today, I am grateful for . . .

My heart's prayer for my child(ren) is . . .

Worries I need to surrender to You . . .

I am feeling overloaded with . . .

Grant me Your unwavering strength for . . .

Fill me with Your wisdom as I seek understanding in . . .

In Jesus's Name. Amen.

God is faithful, by whom you were called
into the fellowship of his Son,
Jesus Christ our Lord.

I Corinthians 1:9 ESV

DATE

Dear God

Today, I am grateful for . . .

My heart's prayer for my child(ren) is . . .

Worries I need to surrender to You . . .

I am feeling overloaded with . . .

Grant me Your unwavering strength for . . .

Fill me with Your wisdom as I seek understanding in . . .

In Jesus's Name. Amen.

Be glad for the chance to suffer as Christ suffered.
It will prepare you for even greater happiness
when He makes His glorious return.

I PETER 4:13 CEV

DATE

Dear God

Today, I am grateful for . . .

My heart's prayer for my child(ren) is . . .

Worries I need to surrender to You . . .

I am feeling overloaded with . . .

Grant me Your unwavering strength for . . .

Fill me with Your wisdom as I seek understanding in . . .

In Jesus's Name. Amen.

For we are God's masterpiece. He has created us anew in Christ Jesus, so we can do the good things He planned for us long ago.

Ephesians 2:10 NLT

DATE

Dear God

Today, I am grateful for . . .

My heart's prayer for my child(ren) is . . .

Worries I need to surrender to You . . .

I am feeling overloaded with . . .

Grant me Your unwavering strength for . . .

Fill me with Your wisdom as I seek understanding in . . .

In Jesus's Name. Amen.

"Fear not, for I am with you; be not dismayed, for I am your God;
I will strengthen you, I will help you, I will uphold you with my righteous right hand."

Isaiah 41:10 esv

First Line of Defense

Our children's lives are changed forever when we pray. God hears our cries. He hears our hearts. Lay your hand on your child each night while they sleep, praying blessings and hope over them, and God hears. Cry out in pain to Him if you see your child making wrong decisions, and He hears. Your heartfelt prayers for protection, or of thanks for who your beautiful child is and is becoming, are heard by God. He delights in them. It strengthens not only your child's life, but also your own relationship with God, when you pray.

The gap between our lips and God's ears is the shortest distance in all creation. And not only does He hear us, but I John 5:14–15 reminds us that when we ask according to His will, we have what we've asked for. We cry out, God hears, and He sees to it.

We may not always be able to be right by their side, holding our child's hand through every circumstance. But we can place our child in God's hands. Through the peace and guidance of His Spirit, our prayers are more effective than any earthly thing we can do.

In the book of Psalms, David dealt with all kinds of emotions. In one verse, David moans and wails to God about his difficult and sometimes painful circumstances, and in the very next verse, David declares his gratitude for his good and faithful and trustworthy God. David knew that he could bring it *all* to God. He knew there was no reason to hide his sorrow from our all-knowing Creator, but he also knew when he cried out, it was more than just beating the sky. He knew there was a mighty God that was listening and understood and cared, and for that, he was grateful. When we, as mothers, are looking to God, let's give ourselves permission to lay it *all* on Him—the stress, anxiety, and frustration. And when He meets us in our dark moments with His loving compassion and indescribable peace, may we always remember to respond with praise.

Prayer is not a last resort. It's a first line of defense for anything you or your family might go through. Perhaps this is a reason that newborns are up at night for feedings and diaper changes? It's an opportunity to put into place the very important habit of praying over your child. There's not much else to do at two in the morning, after all! Throughout your kids' lives, any time you're comforting your child at night or checking on them while they sleep, it's a great time to focus on the sweetness of the precious person you are shepherding. Spend time asking the Lord how to cover your child in prayer. There's literally no better investment you could make from day one.

DATE

Dear God

Today, I am grateful for . . .

My heart's prayer for my child(ren) is . . .

Worries I need to surrender to You . . .

I am feeling overloaded with . . .

Grant me Your unwavering strength for . . .

Fill me with Your wisdom as I seek understanding in . . .

In Jesus's Name. Amen.

I cried out to the LORD; yes, I prayed to my God for help.
He heard me from His sanctuary.

PSALM 18:6 NLT

DATE

Dear God

Today, I am grateful for . . .

My heart's prayer for my child(ren) is . . .

Worries I need to surrender to You . . .

I am feeling overloaded with . . .

Grant me Your unwavering strength for . . .

Fill me with Your wisdom as I seek understanding in . . .

In Jesus's Name. Amen.

So whenever we are in need, we should come bravely before the throne of our merciful God. There we will be treated with undeserved grace, and we will find help.

Hebrews 4:16 CEV

DATE

Dear God

Today, I am grateful for . . .

My heart's prayer for my child(ren) is . . .

Worries I need to surrender to You . . .

I am feeling overloaded with . . .

Grant me Your unwavering strength for . . .

Fill me with Your wisdom as I seek understanding in . . .

In Jesus's Name. Amen.

Rejoice always, pray continually, give thanks in all circumstances; for this is God's will for you in Christ Jesus.

I Thessalonians 5:16–18 niv

DATE

Dear God

Today, I am grateful for . . .

My heart's prayer for my child(ren) is . . .

Worries I need to surrender to You . . .

I am feeling overloaded with . . .

Grant me Your unwavering strength for . . .

Fill me with Your wisdom as I seek understanding in . . .

In Jesus's Name. Amen.

Do not be anxious about anything, but in everything by prayer and supplication with thanksgiving let your requests be made known to God. And the peace of God, which surpasses all understanding, will guard your hearts and your minds in Christ Jesus.

PHILIPPIANS 4:6–7 ESV

DATE

Dear God

Today, I am grateful for . . .

My heart's prayer for my child(ren) is . . .

Worries I need to surrender to You . . .

I am feeling overloaded with . . .

Grant me Your unwavering strength for . . .

Fill me with Your wisdom as I seek understanding in . . .

In Jesus's Name. Amen.

We are certain God will hear our prayers when we ask for what pleases Him.
And if we know God listens when we pray,
we are sure our prayers have already been answered.

I John 5:14–15 CEV

DATE

Dear God

Today, I am grateful for . . .

My heart's prayer for my child(ren) is . . .

Worries I need to surrender to You . . .

I am feeling overloaded with . . .

Grant me Your unwavering strength for . . .

Fill me with Your wisdom as I seek understanding in . . .

In Jesus's Name. Amen.

"Pray like this: Our Father in heaven, may Your name be kept holy.
May Your Kingdom come soon. May Your will be done on earth, as it is in heaven.
Give us today the food we need, and forgive us our sins, as we have forgiven those who sin against us. And don't let us yield to temptation, but rescue us from the evil one."

MATTHEW 6:9–13 NLT

DATE

Dear God

Today, I am grateful for . . .

My heart's prayer for my child(ren) is . . .

Worries I need to surrender to You . . .

I am feeling overloaded with . . .

Grant me Your unwavering strength for . . .

Fill me with Your wisdom as I seek understanding in . . .

In Jesus's Name. Amen.

"Therefore I tell you, whatever you ask for in prayer, believe that you have received it, and it will be yours."

Mark 11:24 niv

Expect God's Best

When parents are "expecting" a baby, they paint nurseries, buy diapers, attend showers, and announce genders. They post ultrasound pictures, deliberate on names, and plan family visits. Life shifts when a woman is "expecting" a new little bundle of joy.

To *expect* is to wait for or look for something. The implication is that the "something" is definitely coming . . . something in the future, something already promised. It's almost as if God says, every time a baby is born, "See, I told you I'm in the miracle business!"

Throughout the Bible, waiting on the Lord is a common theme. But waiting on God is nothing like sitting in a plastic chair, flipping through last month's magazines, and listening to canned music. Waiting on the Lord is meant to be active, hopeful, and exciting. Isaiah 40:31 (NKJV) says that "those who wait on the LORD shall renew their strength; they shall mount up with wings like eagles, they shall run and not be weary, they shall walk and not faint." When God works, which He is doing constantly, the journey is empowering and the results always prove to be worth waiting for.

Babies are the most tangible example of how God is always doing something new in our lives. He gives us dreams, plants the seeds, waters them with time and experience, and allows them to grow to maturity before releasing them into the world. He gives us the tools to live out the vision He has cast for us. We learn, we work with Him, and His glory is revealed.

Whatever God is accomplishing in you, your children only make it a richer, more tangible experience. Expect the very best from God today and in the coming years. Prepare yourself for whatever dreams He's been whispering into your heart—clean up your schedule, tell people you trust, think hopefully and joyfully about what He's unfolding in and through you. He's been planning on this time in your life since time began. In a way, as you wait on Him and expect His very best, He is waiting on you and expecting the great things He has already planned.

DATE

Dear God

Today, I am grateful for . . .

My heart's prayer for my child(ren) is . . .

Worries I need to surrender to You . . .

I am feeling overloaded with . . .

Grant me Your unwavering strength for . . .

Fill me with Your wisdom as I seek understanding in . . .

In Jesus's Name. Amen.

And we know that for those who love God all things work together for good, for those who are called according to his purpose.

Romans 8:28 ESV

DATE

Dear God

Today, I am grateful for . . .

My heart's prayer for my child(ren) is . . .

Worries I need to surrender to You . . .

I am feeling overloaded with . . .

Grant me Your unwavering strength for . . .

Fill me with Your wisdom as I seek understanding in . . .

In Jesus's Name. Amen.

Listen to my voice in the morning, LORD.
Each morning I bring my requests to You and wait expectantly.

PSALM 5:3 NLT

DATE

Dear God

Today, I am grateful for . . .

My heart's prayer for my child(ren) is . . .

Worries I need to surrender to You . . .

I am feeling overloaded with . . .

Grant me Your unwavering strength for . . .

Fill me with Your wisdom as I seek understanding in . . .

In Jesus's Name. Amen.

Now faith is confidence in what we hope for
and assurance about what we do not see.

HEBREWS 11:1 NIV

DATE

Dear God

Today, I am grateful for . . .

My heart's prayer for my child(ren) is . . .

Worries I need to surrender to You . . .

I am feeling overloaded with . . .

Grant me Your unwavering strength for . . .

Fill me with Your wisdom as I seek understanding in . . .

In Jesus's Name. Amen.

Now to him who is able to do far more abundantly than all that we ask or think, according to the power at work within us.

Ephesians 3:20 ESV

DATE

Dear God

Today, I am grateful for . . .

My heart's prayer for my child(ren) is . . .

Worries I need to surrender to You . . .

I am feeling overloaded with . . .

Grant me Your unwavering strength for . . .

Fill me with Your wisdom as I seek understanding in . . .

In Jesus's Name. Amen.

God is the One who began this good work in you,
and I am certain that He won't stop before it is complete
on the day that Christ Jesus returns.

Philippians 1:6 CEV

DATE

Dear God

Today, I am grateful for . . .

My heart's prayer for my child(ren) is . . .

Worries I need to surrender to You . . .

I am feeling overloaded with . . .

Grant me Your unwavering strength for . . .

Fill me with Your wisdom as I seek understanding in . . .

In Jesus's Name. Amen.

Trust in the LORD with all your heart and lean not on your own understanding;
in all your ways submit to Him, and He will make your paths straight.

PROVERBS 3:5–6 NIV

DATE

Today, I am grateful for . . .

My heart's prayer for my child(ren) is . . .

Worries I need to surrender to You . . .

I am feeling overloaded with . . .

Grant me Your unwavering strength for . . .

Fill me with Your wisdom as I seek understanding in . . .

In Jesus's Name. Amen.

It is God who works in you,
both to will and to work for his good pleasure.

PHILIPPIANS 2:13 ESV

Reliable Love

If you ever find yourself dropping a child off at a nursery or school, you'll most likely witness some form of fear and anxiety in some of the children there. Sobs may erupt as the little one realizes he can't see his parents. He remains inconsolable until they return and take him back into their arms. Fortunately, as children mature, they gain a greater understanding of their parents' reliability and deep commitment to them and learn to step away from their fears.

It's not unlike how we walk through our relationship with God. Over and over again on our journey, fear and anxiety can take over as we face new and unknown situations. Take motherhood, for example. So many things we haven't experienced before, so much responsibility seemingly dropped into our laps and new challenges almost every day for years and years—it can be a lot like the first day of school for us, over and over again! And depending on the day, it can very much feel like God has already abandoned us or will if we make the wrong move. It's the mind-set of an infant who doesn't understand the situation. As His beloved children, we are never on the brink of abandonment, despite what our feelings tell us. In fact, even though we may feel like God has left and He's out of our sight, especially when we veer off His prescribed path—His loving hand is still holding us. Before the world was even created, God devised a plan through faith in His Son that would pave a permanent path back to Him no matter what problem besets us.

In his letter to the Ephesians, Paul correlated being deeply rooted in God with being able to understand how incredibly deep, wide, and high His love for us is. Motherhood comes with all kinds of shakings. But the more deeply we burrow ourselves into God's truth and promises, the less shakable we ourselves become. When that report card, diagnosis, or attitude comes along, we will see it through the eyes of eternity and hope. When we need reminding of our ability to do this, our Comforter will come quickly. And as our kids grow, they will see God's truest form of love through our own ability to love them strongly and surely.

Motherhood often brings up a lot of emotions and memories from our own growing-up years. But we can let the panic, shame, misunderstanding, and fear of our younger years go. We are being held, right in this moment. We have a loving Father, our heavenly Daddy, who has made a way for us to belong to Him forever, and He will never leave us, nor will He forsake us.

DATE

Dear God

Today, I am grateful for . . .

My heart's prayer for my child(ren) is . . .

Worries I need to surrender to You . . .

I am feeling overloaded with . . .

Grant me Your unwavering strength for . . .

Fill me with Your wisdom as I seek understanding in . . .

In Jesus's Name. Amen.

I pray that you, being rooted and firmly established in love,
may be able to comprehend with all the saints what is the length and width,
height and depth of God's love.

EPHESIANS 3:17–18 CSB

DATE

Dear God

Today, I am grateful for . . .

My heart's prayer for my child(ren) is . . .

Worries I need to surrender to You . . .

I am feeling overloaded with . . .

Grant me Your unwavering strength for . . .

Fill me with Your wisdom as I seek understanding in . . .

In Jesus's Name. Amen.

So then, just as you received Christ Jesus as Lord,
continue to live your lives in Him, rooted and built up in Him,
strengthened in the faith as you were taught, and overflowing with thankfulness.

Colossians 2:6–7 niv

DATE

Dear God

Today, I am grateful for . . .

My heart's prayer for my child(ren) is . . .

Worries I need to surrender to You . . .

I am feeling overloaded with . . .

Grant me Your unwavering strength for . . .

Fill me with Your wisdom as I seek understanding in . . .

In Jesus's Name. Amen.

And now I entrust you to God and the message of His grace that is able to build you up and give you an inheritance with all those He has set apart for Himself.

Acts 20:32 NLT

DATE

Dear God

Today, I am grateful for . . .

My heart's prayer for my child(ren) is . . .

Worries I need to surrender to You . . .

I am feeling overloaded with . . .

Grant me Your unwavering strength for . . .

Fill me with Your wisdom as I seek understanding in . . .

In Jesus's Name. Amen.

"Abide in Me, and I in you. As the branch cannot bear fruit of itself, unless it abides in the vine, neither can you, unless you abide in Me."

JOHN 15:4 NKJV

DATE

Dear God

Today, I am grateful for . . .

My heart's prayer for my child(ren) is . . .

Worries I need to surrender to You . . .

I am feeling overloaded with . . .

Grant me Your unwavering strength for . . .

Fill me with Your wisdom as I seek understanding in . . .

In Jesus's Name. Amen.

The LORD is my shepherd; I shall not want.

PSALM 23:1 NKJV

DATE

Dear God

Today, I am grateful for . . .

My heart's prayer for my child(ren) is . . .

Worries I need to surrender to You . . .

I am feeling overloaded with . . .

Grant me Your unwavering strength for . . .

Fill me with Your wisdom as I seek understanding in . . .

In Jesus's Name. Amen.

As a father has compassion on his children,
so the LORD has compassion on those who fear Him;
for He knows how we are formed, He remembers that we are dust.

PSALM 103:13–14 NIV

DATE

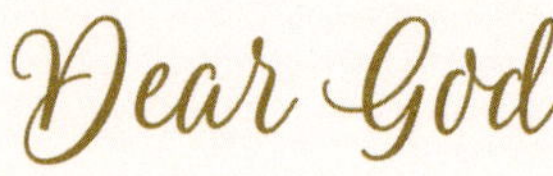

Today, I am grateful for . . .

My heart's prayer for my child(ren) is . . .

Worries I need to surrender to You . . .

I am feeling overloaded with . . .

Grant me Your unwavering strength for . . .

Fill me with Your wisdom as I seek understanding in . . .

In Jesus's Name. Amen.

"Ask Me and I will tell you remarkable secrets
you do not know about things to come."
JEREMIAH 33:3 NLT

Seen, Known, and Valued

You are a mom in your own unique way. No one parent is exactly like you, and for that reason, you are uniquely suited to parent your child. You are the knower of small things, of favorites and things not-so-loved. You can empower with a word. You can heal with a hug. You can calm with a look. At times, you struggle to find power and purpose in what you do. It may seem unimportant and unimpressive. It's easy to look for affirmation that may never come, from husband, kids, coworkers, or friends. It's a good thing we have a God who adores and affirms moms.

We have a God who sees motherhood as a valuable calling and in His wisdom gifts us individually. He delights in you personally. He has paired you and prepared you, equipped you and called you, dressed you in His finest armor to face the day with joy. You have no idea how much you influence your world.

At a time of crisis in Israel, God sent an angel to Gideon (Judges chapters 6–7). Gideon was not standing on a stage somewhere, dying to be seen. He wasn't posting every hour on social media. Gideon was actually hiding, trying to thresh wheat at the bottom of a winepress. He was scared, oppressed, and thoroughly unsure of himself.

But God knew him more deeply. He found

Gideon exactly where he was, gave him exactly what he needed for the task at hand, and told him exactly how to succeed. Gideon didn't understand his value, but God did. And like him, as long as you are responsive to God right where you are, you will thrive as a mom.

God. Delights. In. You. Yep, you. You, who are weary. You, in the office cubicle. You, who diligently serves the less fortunate. You, who loves being a mom. You are beloved to Him. God delights in His children. The end.

When you feel the weight of not knowing whether you make a difference . . . when you feel the tedium of another day of the same things over and over . . . when you feel the heat of trying to do the very best you can for your family . . . God sees it all, and He reassures you: "Count it all joy, child. I see you. I know you. I can't wait for you to feel the warmth of My acceptance of you in all its fullness. In the meantime, take comfort in the peace that passes understanding. You are right where you belong—in this home, with this family, and in My heart."

DATE

Dear God

Today, I am grateful for . . .

My heart's prayer for my child(ren) is . . .

Worries I need to surrender to You . . .

I am feeling overloaded with . . .

Grant me Your unwavering strength for . . .

Fill me with Your wisdom as I seek understanding in . . .

In Jesus's Name. Amen.

See what great love the Father has lavished on us,
that we should be called children of God!

I John 3:1 NIV

DATE

Dear God

Today, I am grateful for . . .

My heart's prayer for my child(ren) is . . .

Worries I need to surrender to You . . .

I am feeling overloaded with . . .

Grant me Your unwavering strength for . . .

Fill me with Your wisdom as I seek understanding in . . .

In Jesus's Name. Amen.

Count it all joy, my brothers, when you meet trials of various kinds,
for you know that the testing of your faith produces steadfastness.

JAMES 1:2–3 ESV

DATE

Today, I am grateful for . . .

My heart's prayer for my child(ren) is . . .

Worries I need to surrender to You . . .

I am feeling overloaded with . . .

Grant me Your unwavering strength for . . .

Fill me with Your wisdom as I seek understanding in . . .

In Jesus's Name. Amen.

"But Lord," Gideon replied, "how can I rescue Israel? My clan is the weakest in the whole tribe of Manasseh, and I am the least in my entire family!" The LORD said to him, "I will be with you. And you will destroy the Midianites as if you were fighting against one man."

JUDGES 6:15–16 NLT

DATE

Dear God

Today, I am grateful for . . .

My heart's prayer for my child(ren) is . . .

Worries I need to surrender to You . . .

I am feeling overloaded with . . .

Grant me Your unwavering strength for . . .

Fill me with Your wisdom as I seek understanding in . . .

In Jesus's Name. Amen.

Keep your minds on whatever is true, pure, right, holy, friendly, and proper . . .
You know the teachings I gave you, and you know what you heard me say and saw me do.
So follow my example. And God, who gives peace, will be with you.

PHILIPPIANS 4:8–9 CEV

DATE

Dear God

Today, I am grateful for . . .

My heart's prayer for my child(ren) is . . .

Worries I need to surrender to You . . .

I am feeling overloaded with . . .

Grant me Your unwavering strength for . . .

Fill me with Your wisdom as I seek understanding in . . .

In Jesus's Name. Amen.

"You are precious in my eyes,
and honored, and I love you."

Isaiah 43:4 ESV

DATE

Dear God

Today, I am grateful for . . .

My heart's prayer for my child(ren) is . . .

Worries I need to surrender to You . . .

I am feeling overloaded with . . .

Grant me Your unwavering strength for . . .

Fill me with Your wisdom as I seek understanding in . . .

In Jesus's Name. Amen.

But He said to me, "My grace is sufficient for you,
for My power is made perfect in weakness."

II CORINTHIANS 12:9 NIV

DATE

Dear God

Today, I am grateful for . . .

My heart's prayer for my child(ren) is . . .

Worries I need to surrender to You . . .

I am feeling overloaded with . . .

Grant me Your unwavering strength for . . .

Fill me with Your wisdom as I seek understanding in . . .

In Jesus's Name. Amen.

"Are not five sparrows sold for two pennies? And not one of them is forgotten before God.
Why, even the hairs of your head are all numbered.
Fear not; you are of more value than many sparrows."

Luke 12:6–7 ESV

Let's Do This Together

Throughout your child's growing-up years, you've likely experienced (and will continue to experience) a sense that you just can't do it alone. The sting of loneliness is very real and doesn't always follow the logic: your husband may be supportive, your family may live nearby, you follow all the experts, and you see other moms at the local park. But still, the desire to be known can punch you in the gut like a ten-year-old running too fast around the corner. And that's if you do have all of those sources of connection. If you're a single mom or live away from family, that can be whole other level of tough.

You may find that you need someone else to look you in the eyes and say, "I didn't sleep last night either." Or show up at your house in a spit up–stained shirt. Then you could point to your own shirt (the one you'd slept in for the last two nights), and you could commiserate together. You might be craving the companionship of others with whom you can walk down the road of motherhood. Because there's just something about facing the same fears in the same moment with people who really see you. If this is you, then pray: *Lord Jesus, please bring me friends*. And He will.

In between the diaper changes, the meal fixing, the mom taxiing, the exhaustion, and the joy, friendship will form. Jesus-joined hearts will always walk life together, making it stronger. Because that's what friendship does. We were never meant to travel this life without the refuge of friends.

Galatians 6:2 expressly says that we are here to bear one another's burdens. Sometimes that means the heaviest grief, loss, or illness. Most of the time, though, our burdens look a lot more ordinary. The weariness of the mundane can be broken with one girls' night out or by finding an early morning workout buddy. Having friends who truly care about you makes a huge difference in going through life with joy and contentment.

Life lived in relationships allows us to survive the deep end. We can test the waters alone, wading out a bit by ourselves, but if we must head to the deep places of life, we need friends to keep the ocean from swallowing us whole. Each friendship can serve as a lifeline, tethering us to the shore when our circumstances try to suck us under.

In His great mercy and grace, our Jesus has given us the gift of friendship. And if you're in the space, ankle-deep headed toward the dark waters, pray for hands to hold you steady. Pray and ask our Holy One for kindred spirits to walk beside you in this journey. Because the drowning only comes when we attempt to travel alone.

DATE

Dear God

Today, I am grateful for . . .

My heart's prayer for my child(ren) is . . .

Worries I need to surrender to You . . .

I am feeling overloaded with . . .

Grant me Your unwavering strength for . . .

Fill me with Your wisdom as I seek understanding in . . .

In Jesus's Name. Amen.

Encourage one another and build each other up,
just as in fact you are doing.

I THESSALONIANS 5:11 NIV

DATE

Dear God

Today, I am grateful for . . .

My heart's prayer for my child(ren) is . . .

Worries I need to surrender to You . . .

I am feeling overloaded with . . .

Grant me Your unwavering strength for . . .

Fill me with Your wisdom as I seek understanding in . . .

In Jesus's Name. Amen.

Let us consider how to stir up one another to love and good works,
not neglecting to meet together, as is the habit of some, but encouraging one another.

Hebrews 10:24–25 esv

DATE

Dear God

Today, I am grateful for . . .

My heart's prayer for my child(ren) is . . .

Worries I need to surrender to You . . .

I am feeling overloaded with . . .

Grant me Your unwavering strength for . . .

Fill me with Your wisdom as I seek understanding in . . .

In Jesus's Name. Amen.

Share each other's burdens,
and in this way obey the law of Christ.

GALATIANS 6:2 NLT

DATE

Dear God

Today, I am grateful for . . .

My heart's prayer for my child(ren) is . . .

Worries I need to surrender to You . . .

I am feeling overloaded with . . .

Grant me Your unwavering strength for . . .

Fill me with Your wisdom as I seek understanding in . . .

In Jesus's Name. Amen.

As each one has received a gift, minister it to one another,
as good stewards of the manifold grace of God.

I PETER 4:10 NKJV

DATE

Dear God

Today, I am grateful for . . .

My heart's prayer for my child(ren) is . . .

Worries I need to surrender to You . . .

I am feeling overloaded with . . .

Grant me Your unwavering strength for . . .

Fill me with Your wisdom as I seek understanding in . . .

In Jesus's Name. Amen.

Two are better than one, because they have a good return for their labor:
If either of them falls down, one can help the other up.

ECCLESIASTES 4:9–10 NIV

DATE

Dear God

Today, I am grateful for . . .

My heart's prayer for my child(ren) is . . .

Worries I need to surrender to You . . .

I am feeling overloaded with . . .

Grant me Your unwavering strength for . . .

Fill me with Your wisdom as I seek understanding in . . .

In Jesus's Name. Amen.

"Greater love has no one than this,
that someone lay down his life for his friends."
JOHN 15:13 ESV

DATE

Dear God

Today, I am grateful for . . .

My heart's prayer for my child(ren) is . . .

Worries I need to surrender to You . . .

I am feeling overloaded with . . .

Grant me Your unwavering strength for . . .

Fill me with Your wisdom as I seek understanding in . . .

In Jesus's Name. Amen.

"Do to others as you
would like them to do to you."

LUKE 6:31 NLT

Stop and Smell the Moments

There's one thing about becoming a mother that no one talks about much: the time warp. Somehow, once your daughter or son enters the picture, time utterly slows down in your home—while it speeds up everywhere else. Just watch social media: the world moves on, your friends start having all the fun, the new smartphone comes out, stand-up paddle boarding becomes all the rage, and the best movies hit the theaters. Meanwhile, you're home. Holding a baby. Feeding a baby. Changing a baby. Burping a baby. Trying to get a shower. Over. And over. And over again. Every day. All night. Yes, kids are just wonderful! But at the same time, your house suddenly seems to reflect the movie *Groundhog Day*, while everyone else is having the time of their lives. Certainly, the term FOMO ("fear of missing out") was birthed out of a home with a frazzled mom watching the world go by without her.

But catch that truth up there about three-quarters of the way through: kids are wonderful. Each child is a gift to the world, to your home, and to your heart. And if he or she is a gift from God (which is most certainly true), then having children comes with benefits beyond compare. Maybe—just maybe—it's the world that misses out. Maybe the world needs to sit down and stick its nose into the soft folds of a newborn's neck. Maybe the world needs to run its lips gently across tiny baby toes. Maybe the world needs to take the week off and spend each afternoon with its arms wrapped around a tired toddler who finally gave up and fell asleep on the world's chest, feeling the quick little breaths on its cheek and listening to the softest sounds of an innocent, tiny dreamer so close.

Maybe the world has forgotten how to relish life. And maybe you, with your schedule centered on soccer practice and homework and playdates, are the stuff of envy. And maybe the world knows it. Maybe the world will try to convince you to be more like it, when you have every right to whisper from underneath the covers while reading a bedtime story "Come sit. Enjoy this moment. Really, really enjoy it. Don't let it slip past unnoticed."

Contentment comes in all shapes and sizes, and God knows. He planned it that way, handpicking the gifts that would land like birthday presents in your heart throughout your whole life. Your kids are, arguably, the very best things that will ever happen to you—even when it doesn't feel that way. Make sure you pause often, breathing in the sights and smells of this season and enjoying the precious ones whom God has placed under your special and valuable care.

DATE

Dear God

Today, I am grateful for . . .

My heart's prayer for my child(ren) is . . .

Worries I need to surrender to You . . .

I am feeling overloaded with . . .

Grant me Your unwavering strength for . . .

Fill me with Your wisdom as I seek understanding in . . .

In Jesus's Name. Amen.

Every good gift and every perfect gift is from above,
and comes down from the Father.

JAMES 1:17 NKJV

DATE

Dear God

Today, I am grateful for . . .

My heart's prayer for my child(ren) is . . .

Worries I need to surrender to You . . .

I am feeling overloaded with . . .

Grant me Your unwavering strength for . . .

Fill me with Your wisdom as I seek understanding in . . .

In Jesus's Name. Amen.

I take pleasure in my weaknesses, and in the insults, hardships, persecutions, and troubles that I suffer for Christ. For when I am weak, then I am strong.

II Corinthians 12:10 NLT

DATE

Dear God

Today, I am grateful for . . .

My heart's prayer for my child(ren) is . . .

Worries I need to surrender to You . . .

I am feeling overloaded with . . .

Grant me Your unwavering strength for . . .

Fill me with Your wisdom as I seek understanding in . . .

In Jesus's Name. Amen.

The LORD God is my strength;
He will make my feet like deer's feet,
and He will make me walk on my high hills.

HABAKKUK 3:19 NKJV

DATE

Dear God

Today, I am grateful for . . .

My heart's prayer for my child(ren) is . . .

Worries I need to surrender to You . . .

I am feeling overloaded with . . .

Grant me Your unwavering strength for . . .

Fill me with Your wisdom as I seek understanding in . . .

In Jesus's Name. Amen.

Let us not become weary in doing good,
for at the proper time we will reap a harvest if we do not give up.

GALATIANS 6:9 NIV

DATE

Dear God

Today, I am grateful for . . .

My heart's prayer for my child(ren) is . . .

Worries I need to surrender to You . . .

I am feeling overloaded with . . .

Grant me Your unwavering strength for . . .

Fill me with Your wisdom as I seek understanding in . . .

In Jesus's Name. Amen.

Let us hold fast the confession of our hope without wavering,
for he who promised is faithful.

HEBREWS 10:23 ESV

DATE

Dear God

Today, I am grateful for . . .

My heart's prayer for my child(ren) is . . .

Worries I need to surrender to You . . .

I am feeling overloaded with . . .

Grant me Your unwavering strength for . . .

Fill me with Your wisdom as I seek understanding in . . .

In Jesus's Name. Amen.

Yet I am confident I will see the LORD's goodness
while I am here in the land of the living.

PSALM 27:13 NLT

DATE

Dear God

Today, I am grateful for . . .

My heart's prayer for my child(ren) is . . .

Worries I need to surrender to You . . .

I am feeling overloaded with . . .

Grant me Your unwavering strength for . . .

Fill me with Your wisdom as I seek understanding in . . .

In Jesus's Name. Amen.

And my God shall supply all your need
according to His riches in glory by Christ Jesus.

PHILIPPIANS 4:19 NKJV

Your Prayers Matter

It's easy for us, as moms and earthly people fully responsible for our little ones, to forget that God is actually the One in charge. He formulated your child's DNA. He programmed body type, likes and dislikes, gifts and talents, and so much more. A baby doesn't need to be built from the ground up by his or her parents. Instead, a baby needs parents who will observe the person God already created him or her to be. Children need parents who will champion their strengths, love them through their weaknesses, and train them to keep their eyes on Jesus.

That is *not* to minimize the work of a mother in the life of a child. A mom makes an infinite number of decisions that will affect her children's growth and development throughout their lifetimes. But the primary role of a mother is to love—and to pray.

Psalm 62:8 promises that God is the trustworthy destination for our heart's desires. When a mom needs a place to rest, hide, seek truth and direction, and pour out everything she's feeling—God is the place and Person. He actually wants us to come to Him with everything. And He has just the right thing to say at just the right time.

Pray that your son or daughter will know God on the deepest level. Pray that as your child grows, they will learn to separate the truth from the lies. Ask God how to pray for your child and follow

His lead. You'll find that shepherding, training, and loving your children is one of the best opportunities for your own growth in the Lord!

Your child is a person who has been so meticulously planned by the Maker of the universe. He designed the color of her eyes to go with the shape of her face. He appointed that smile, those fingers, that color of hair. Instead of worrying, spend your time marveling at the creation on your lap. And marvel at the fact that God is asking you to partner with Him to raise this little one up.

You yourself were chosen by God, loved by Him, and designed in great detail. He knew your name before you were even a thought in your own mother's mind. Likewise, your child is just as loved and known.

DATE

Dear God

Today, I am grateful for . . .

My heart's prayer for my child(ren) is . . .

Worries I need to surrender to You . . .

I am feeling overloaded with . . .

Grant me Your unwavering strength for . . .

Fill me with Your wisdom as I seek understanding in . . .

In Jesus's Name. Amen.

I call to You, LORD, come quickly to me; hear me when I call to You.
May my prayer be set before You like incense;
may the lifting up of my hands be like the evening sacrifice.

PSALM 141:1–2 NIV

DATE

Today, I am grateful for . . .

My heart's prayer for my child(ren) is . . .

Worries I need to surrender to You . . .

I am feeling overloaded with . . .

Grant me Your unwavering strength for . . .

Fill me with Your wisdom as I seek understanding in . . .

In Jesus's Name. Amen.

Seek the LORD and his strength;
seek his presence continually!
I CHRONICLES 16:11 ESV

DATE

Dear God

Today, I am grateful for . . .

My heart's prayer for my child(ren) is . . .

Worries I need to surrender to You . . .

I am feeling overloaded with . . .

Grant me Your unwavering strength for . . .

Fill me with Your wisdom as I seek understanding in . . .

In Jesus's Name. Amen.

And pray in the Spirit on all occasions with all kinds of prayers and requests. With this in mind, be alert and always keep on praying for all the Lord's people.

Ephesians 6:18 niv

DATE

Dear God

Today, I am grateful for . . .

My heart's prayer for my child(ren) is . . .

Worries I need to surrender to You . . .

I am feeling overloaded with . . .

Grant me Your unwavering strength for . . .

Fill me with Your wisdom as I seek understanding in . . .

In Jesus's Name. Amen.

Never stop praying.

I THESSALONIANS 5:17 NLT

DATE

Dear God

Today, I am grateful for . . .

My heart's prayer for my child(ren) is . . .

Worries I need to surrender to You . . .

I am feeling overloaded with . . .

Grant me Your unwavering strength for . . .

Fill me with Your wisdom as I seek understanding in . . .

In Jesus's Name. Amen.

The earnest prayer of a righteous person has
great power and produces wonderful results.

James 5:16 NLT

DATE

Dear God

Today, I am grateful for . . .

My heart's prayer for my child(ren) is . . .

Worries I need to surrender to You . . .

I am feeling overloaded with . . .

Grant me Your unwavering strength for . . .

Fill me with Your wisdom as I seek understanding in . . .

In Jesus's Name. Amen.

All your children shall be taught by the LORD,
and great shall be the peace of your children.

ISAIAH 54:13 NKJV

DATE

Dear God

Today, I am grateful for . . .

My heart's prayer for my child(ren) is . . .

Worries I need to surrender to You . . .

I am feeling overloaded with . . .

Grant me Your unwavering strength for . . .

Fill me with Your wisdom as I seek understanding in . . .

In Jesus's Name. Amen.

But grow in the grace and knowledge of our Lord and Savior Jesus Christ.
To him be the glory both now and to the day of eternity.

II Peter 3:18 esv

The Comfort Promises by DaySpring™

No matter what you are facing today, you can rest in knowing the Creator of the universe loves you. He loves you deeply and perfectly with absolutely no conditions. And He's made hundreds of promises to you!

Below you'll find the 100 most referenced, quoted, and memorized Bible promises. At DaySpring, we call these The Comfort Promises™—the verses we turn to again and again for encouragement, joy, and strength.

For your convenience, we've provided a quick reference guide—a unique tool that makes it easy for you to find just the right comfort promises for your immediate need.

When you are AFRAID . . .

He will not allow
your foot to slip;
He who keeps you
will not slumber.

PSALM 121:3 NASB1995

"Do not fear; I will help you."

ISAIAH 41:13 NIV

Draw near to God,
and He will draw near to you.

JAMES 4:8 CSB

When you are ANXIOUS . . .

"If you follow Me, you won't have to walk in darkness, because you will have the light that leads to life."

JOHN 8:12 NLT

Don't fret or worry.
Instead of worrying, pray.

PHILIPPIANS 4:6 THE MESSAGE

He never changes or
casts a shifting shadow.

JAMES 1:17 NLT

When you need ASSURANCE . . .

He is the faithful God,
keeping His covenant of love
to a thousand generations.
DEUTERONOMY 7:9 NIV

"You're blessed when you're
at the end of your rope.
With less of you
there is more of God."
MATTHEW 5:3 THE MESSAGE

He chose us . . .
that we would be
holy and blameless before Him.
EPHESIANS 1:4 NASB1995

You are saved by grace
through faith . . .
it is God's gift.
EPHESIANS 2:8 CSB

He cares about you.
I PETER 5:7 NLT

His divine power
has given us everything
required for life.
II PETER 1:3 CSB

When you need COMFORT . . .

The LORD is near the
brokenhearted;
He saves those
crushed in spirit.
PSALM 34:18 CSB

Take delight in the LORD,
and He will give you
your heart's desires.
PSALM 37:4 CSB

"My faithful love for you will
remain. My covenant of blessing
will never be broken."
ISAIAH 54:10 NLT

"I have it all planned out—
plans to take care of you,
not abandon you, plans to
give you the future you hope for."
JEREMIAH 29:11 THE MESSAGE

He will rejoice over you with
gladness. . . . He will delight
in you with singing.
ZEPHANIAH 3:17 CSB

When you need COMFORT (cont'd) . . .

"Blessed are those who mourn,
for they shall be comforted."
MATTHEW 5:4 ESV

He comforts us
in all our troubles
so that we can comfort others.
II CORINTHIANS 1:4 NLT

God has chosen you
and made you
His holy people.
He loves you.
COLOSSIANS 3:12 ICB

When you need COURAGE . . .

But You, LORD, are a shield
around me, my glory,
and the One who
lifts up my head.
PSALM 3:3 CSB

I can do all things
through Christ because
He gives me strength.
PHILIPPIANS 4:13 ICB

He hears their cry
for help and saves them.
PSALM 145:19 CSB

"I will strengthen you,
I will help you,
I will uphold you
with my righteous right hand."
ISAIAH 41:10 ESV

This is what the LORD says,
He who made the earth,
the LORD who formed it and
established it—the LORD is
His name: "Call to Me and I will
answer you and tell you
great and unsearchable
things you do not know."
JEREMIAH 33:2–3 NIV

The LORD is good to
those who wait for Him,
to the person who seeks Him.
LAMENTATIONS 3:25 NASB1995

"I will send you the Helper
from the Father.
He is the Spirit of truth
who comes from the Father."
JOHN 15:26 ICB

He hears us.
I JOHN 5:14 NASB

When you need HOPE . . .

The Lord will fight
for you, while you keep silent.
Exodus 14:14 NASB

Be strong; don't give up,
for your work has a reward.
II Chronicles 15:7 CSB

The Lord grants
favor and honor;
He does not withhold
the good from those
who live with integrity.
Psalm 84:11 CSB

He has planted eternity
in the human heart.
Ecclesiastes 3:11 NLT

His mercies never end.
They are new every morning.
Lamentations 3:22–23 CSB

"I am the living bread. . . .
Whoever eats this bread
will live forever."
John 6:51 NIV

"Anyone who
believes in Me will live,
even after dying."
John 11:25 NLT

We have this hope
as an anchor for the soul,
firm and secure.
Hebrews 6:19 NIV

When you need JOY . . .

Do not grieve,
for the joy of the Lord
is your strength.
Nehemiah 8:10 NIV

You will fill me with joy
in Your presence.
Psalm 16:11 NIV

You turned my lament
into dancing.
Psalm 30:11 CSB

"Give, and it will
be given to you."
Luke 6:38 NIV

When you are LONELY . . .

He will be with you;
He will not leave you
or abandon you.
DEUTERONOMY 31:8 CSB

The LORD your God
is with you wherever you go.
JOSHUA 1:9 CSB

He Himself has said,
"I will never leave you
or abandon you."
HEBREWS 13:5 CSB

When you are feeling OVERWHELMED . . .

"For nothing will be
impossible with God."
LUKE 1:37 ESV

The God of all grace . . .
will himself restore, confirm,
strengthen, and establish you.
I PETER 5:10 ESV

When you need PEACE . . .

The LORD gives
His people strength;
the LORD blesses
His people with peace.
PSALM 29:11 CSB

"Peace I leave with you.
My peace I give to you."
JOHN 14:27 CSB

God's peace will keep
your hearts and minds
in Christ Jesus.
PHILIPPIANS 4:7 ICB

When you need PROTECTION . . .

You are a hiding place
for me;
you preserve me
from trouble.
PSALM 32:7 ESV

You protect people
as a bird protects
her young under her wings.
PSALM 36:7 ICB

God has not given us
a spirit of fear,
but one of power, love,
and sound judgment.
II TIMOTHY 1:7 CSB

Humble yourselves
before the Lord,
and He will lift you up.
JAMES 4:10 NIV

When you need ENCOURAGEMENT . . .

His faithful love
endures forever.
PSALM 100:5 CSB

"I will give you
a new heart
and put a new spirit
within you."
EZEKIEL 36:26 CSB

For I am convinced
that neither death nor life,
neither angels nor demons,
neither the present nor the future,
nor any powers, neither height
nor depth, nor anything else
in all creation, will be able
to separate us from
the love of God that is
in Christ Jesus our Lord.
ROMANS 8:38–39 NIV

He will not let you be
tempted beyond your ability.
I CORINTHIANS 10:13 ESV

He has created us anew
in Christ Jesus, so we can do
the good things He planned for us.
EPHESIANS 2:10 NLT

When you need FORGIVENESS . . .

"I will forgive their sin
and will heal their land."
II Chronicles 7:14 NIV

"Though your
sins are scarlet,
they will be
as white as snow."
Isaiah 1:18 CSB

By giving Himself completely
at the Cross, actually dying
for you, Christ brought
you over to God's side
and put your lives together,
whole and holy in His presence.
Colossians 1:22 The Message

He . . . will forgive
us our sins
and purify us.
I John 1:9 NIV

God . . . will bring you
with great joy
into His glorious presence
without a single fault.
Jude 1:24 NLT

When you need GUIDANCE . . .

He will make
your paths straight.
Proverbs 3:6 CSB

The Lord will
continually guide you.
Isaiah 58:11 NASB1995

"When the Spirit
of truth comes,
He will guide you
into all truth."
John 16:13 NLT

When you need HEALING . . .

He heals the brokenhearted and
binds up their wounds.
Psalm 147:3 ESV

By His wounds
we are healed.
Isaiah 53:5 NIV

"I will give you back
your health and heal
your wounds."
Jeremiah 30:17 NLT

When you need HELP . . .

"I will send you rain in its season,
and the ground will yield its crops
and the trees their fruit."
LEVITICUS 26:4 NIV

Day after day
He bears our burdens.
PSALM 68:19 CSB

He will give His angels orders . . .
to protect you in all your ways.
PSALM 91:11 CSB

The LORD will guard your
going out and your coming in from
this time forth and forever.
PSALM 121:8 NASB1995

He is a shield to those
who take refuge in Him.
PROVERBS 30:5 CSB

A stronghold for the poor . . .
a refuge from storms
and a shade from heat.
ISAIAH 25:4 CSB

No weapon turned
against you will succeed.
ISAIAH 54:17 NLT

He will strengthen
you and protect you.
II THESSALONIANS 3:3 NIV

When you need REST and RENEWAL . . .

The LORD is my shepherd,
I lack nothing. He makes me lie
down in green pastures, He leads
me beside quiet waters.
PSALM 23:1–2 NIV

He renews my life;
He leads me along the
right paths for His name's sake.
PSALM 23:3 CSB

He satisfies you with good things;
your youth is renewed
like the eagle.
PSALM 103:5 CSB

Those who wait for
the LORD will gain
new strength;
they will mount up
with wings like eagles,
they will run and not get tired,
they will walk
and not become weary.
ISAIAH 40:31 NASB1995

When you need REST and RENEWAL (cont'd) . . .

"Come to me, all who
labor and are heavy laden,
and I will give you rest."

Matthew 11:28 ESV

"The Son of Man came
to find and restore the lost."

Luke 19:10 The Message

Jesus answered,
"Everyone who drinks
this water will be thirsty again,
but whoever drinks the water
I give them will never thirst.
Indeed, the water I give them
will become in them
a spring of water welling up
to eternal life."

John 4:13–14 NIV

Our inner person is being
renewed day by day.

II Corinthians 4:16 CSB

If anyone is in Christ,
he is a new creation.

II Corinthians 5:17 CSB

When you need STRENGTH . . .

He gives power to the weak and
strength to the powerless.

Isaiah 40:29 NLT

The Spirit helps us in our
weakness.

Romans 8:26 ESV

He will keep you strong
to the end so that you will be free
from all blame on the day when
our Lord Jesus Christ returns.

I Corinthians 1:8 NLT

When you are SUFFERING . . .

He will sustain you;
He will never allow
the righteous to be shaken.

Psalm 55:22 NASB1995

As a father has compassion on
his children, so the Lord has
compassion on those who fear Him;
for He knows how we are formed,
He remembers that we are dust.

Psalm 103:13–14 NIV

"I will be with you. . . .
When you walk
through the fire,
you will not be scorched."

Isaiah 43:2 CSB

"I will be your God
throughout your lifetime—
until your hair is white with age."

Isaiah 46:4 NLT

The Lord is good,
a stronghold
in the day of trouble.

Nahum 1:7 ESV

"Remain in Me,
and I will remain in you."

John 15:4 NLT

When you need WISDOM . . .

"Continue to ask,
and God will give to you.
Continue to search,
and you will find.
Continue to knock,
and the door will open for you."

Matthew 7:7 ICB

It is because of Him
that you are in Christ Jesus,
who has become for us
wisdom from God—that is,
our righteousness,
holiness and redemption.

I Corinthians 1:30 NIV

Now if any of you lacks wisdom,
he should ask God . . .
and it will be given to him.

James 1:5 CSB

When you are WORRIED . . .

"Your Father knows
the things you need
before you ask Him."

Matthew 6:8 ICB

God will meet
all your needs.

Philippians 4:19 NIV

Prayer Journal for Moms

First Edition, March 2024

Published by:

21154 Highway 16 East
Siloam Springs, AR 72761
dayspring.com

Written by: Trieste Vaillancourt
Cover Design: Becca Barnett

Printed in Vietnam
Prime: U1229
ISBN: 979-8-88602-412-8